Edward Gibbon's

The History of the Decline and Fall of the Roman Empire

T0351398

the Emperors of Germany, and Kings
of Spain have threatened the liberty
of the old, and invaded the treasures
of the new, World The successors of
Charles the fifth to may disdain their
humble kinsmen of England: but the
small volumes of Tom Jones, that
exquisite picture of human life
will survive the palace of the Escurial
of the the and the Imperial eagle of the
house of Austria.

GIBBON'S HANDWRITING, circa 1790 [ITEM 9]

Edward Gibbon's

The History of the Decline and Fall of the Roman Empire

---

*Illustrated by Treasures in the
Chapin Library at Williams College*

*An exhibition at Williams College
on the occasion of a visit by*

THE GROLIER CLUB

XI NOVEMBER MM

CONTENTS

☙

INTRODUCTION

P RACTICALLY ALL OF THE BOOKS in this exhibition are from the Chapin Library at Williams College. The three items that actually passed through the hands of Edward Gibbon were lent especially for the exhibition: these are the first edition of Volume I of *The History of the Decline and Fall of the Roman Empire*, which is in its original binding, that is a presentation copy from Gibbon to Lord Sandys (ITEM 1); the fragment of Gibbon's autobiography that is in his handwriting (ITEM 9); and the book from his library that contains his bookplates (ITEM 14).

According to Lucy Eugenia Osborne, who prepared a short-title list of the collection, Alfred Clark Chapin (1848-1936) began in 1915 to collect rare books as a gift for Williams College. Beginning with a perfect copy of the Eliot Indian Bible of 1661, Mr. Chapin continued to buy, building up as the three main divisions, Incunabula, English Literature, and Americana. These were supplemented by continental literature after 1500, bibles and liturgies, early manuscripts, science, ballads and broadsides, and illustrated books. In the course of eight years some nine thousand volumes were acquired, and in that year, 1923, they were presented to the President and Trustees of Williams. Since Mr. Chapin (Class of 1869) was governed by a determination to secure books in fine condition, his gift to his Alma Mater comprises distinguished copies from such great libraries as the Hoe, Huth, Britwell, Pembroke, Amherst, and Vernon. The acquiring of rare books was one of his great pleasures, for he hoped that the Library would fall naturally into place in the life of the College.

Subsequent to the original gift, many more books were added and the Library continues to collect and to mount exhibitions from its collections, including one to complement the neighboring Clark Art Institute's recent exhibition, "Orientalism in America, 1870-1930."

❀

O<small>N PERMANENT DISPLAY</small>, the Chapin has copies of the founding documents for the American Republic, including "first editions" of the *Declaration of Independence* and the *Constitution*, and George Washington's copy of *The Federalist*. For this exhibition, they provide a contemporary background for the publication of Gibbon's *Decline and Fall* from February 17, 1776 through June 9, 1788.

Edward Gibbon was a gentleman scholar and an avid bookman but he was not particularly interested in collecting rarities. The first editions in his library of over six thousand volumes were by contemporaries such as Henry Fielding, Adam Smith, and William Blackstone. As for his collection as a whole, he could have said of himself what he wrote in describing the emperor Gordian II (circa AD 238): his library was "designed for use rather than ostentation." Gibbon knew the history of the book well; for example, the work of Aldus Manutius and the Florentine Homer of 1488, which are in the Chapin but not in Gibbon's library, are cited in the footnotes of the *Decline and Fall*. The *titles* that were in Gibbon's library, however, do provide an opportunity to show off the *treasures* in the Chapin.

I discovered the Chapin Library when my daughter, Elizabeth '85, was an undergraduate at Williams. Since then it has been my "dream library" because the Aldines and the early Greek and English bibles that I coveted during my collecting days were already there. From my first visit, I was made most welcome by Robert Volz, the Custodian, and Wayne Hammond, the Assistant Librarian. They are the ones who encouraged a visit from the Grolier Club and they must be congratulated for the real work of mounting the books for display. The

Classics Department of the College also welcomed the exhibition and kindly lent the ancient Roman coins from their archives. Independently, G. W. Bowersock, Professor of Ancient History at the Institute for Advanced Study in Princeton, suggested "Gibbon's Library" for his talk on Gibbon. That happy coincidence bodes well for our visit.

GEORGE EDWARDS

THE EXHIBITION

I • 1776 – A Year of Three Classics in Caslon

"The first Volume of my History of the decline and fall of the Roman Empire was published." — Entry in Edward Gibbon's pocket diary for Saturday, February 17, 1776.

The type fonts designed by William Caslon (1692-1766) were used for Edward Gibbon's *Decline and Fall of the Roman Empire*, Adam Smith's *Wealth of Nations,* and Thomas Jefferson's *Declaration of Independence.* [See one of the first copies of the *Declaration* in the display case.]

1   **Edward Gibbon (1737-1794), *The History of the Decline and Fall of the Roman Empire*, Vol. I. London, for W. Strahan and T. Cadell, February 1776.** FIRST EDITION.
(From the collection of Helmut N. Friedlaender)

In original boards. Copies were issued by the publisher in this style binding at a price of one guinea (21 shillings). Drab grey boards were also used for the publisher's bindings for Vols. II & III (1781) and Vols. IV-VI (1788). The price for the complete set was £6. 6s. (one guinea a volume).

2   **Edward Gibbon (1737-1794), *The History of the Decline and Fall of the Roman Empire*, Vol. I. London, for W. Strahan and T. Cadell, February 1776.** FIRST EDITION.

The original impression for Vol. I was planned for 750 and then reduced to only 500 copies; however, the printer Strahan became optimistic part-way through the print run and the edition was expanded to 1000. It is easy to identify the first 500 because the printer took the opportunity to correct the errata as far as page 208 of the text in the second 500 copies. Pages 1-208 in this particular copy are from the initial run. The engraving, dated February 1780, is by John Hall from Joshua Reynold's portrait of Gibbon painted in

1779. It was first issued separately and was published as the frontispiece for Vol. II of the *Decline and Fall* in 1781, but is often found bound in Vol. I.

3 **Adam Smith (1723-1790), *An Inquiry into the Nature and Causes of the Wealth of Nations*. London, for W. Strahan and T. Cadell, March 1776. 2 vols. FIRST EDITION.**

Adam Smith's *Wealth of Nations* was published shortly after the publication of the *Decline and Fall*, also by Strahan, printer, and Cadell, bookseller, and in Caslon type. Although not as popular as the *Decline and Fall*, it too achieved classic status. (See the Grolier Club's *One Hundred Books Famous in English Literature*, 1903.) Gibbon and Adam Smith were good friends: "This last [Smith's Inquiry into the Nature and Causes of the Wealth of Nations] I am proud to quote, as the work of a sage and a friend." — *Decline and Fall*, CHAP. XXIX, NOTE 15.

II · Contemporary Opinions

"Lo there has just appeared a truly classic work . . . Mr. Gibbon's History of the Decline and Fall of the Roman Empire." — Horace Walpole
in a letter to the Rev. William Mason, February 18, 1776.

4 **Horace Walpole (1717-1797), *The Mysterious Mother, a Tragedy*. Strawberry-Hill 1768. FIRST EDITION.**

In the same letter in which Horace Walpole dubbed the *Decline and Fall* a "classic" — on the day after publication — he goes on: "Do I know nothing superior to Mr. Gibbon? Yes . . . Mr. Gibbon's are good sense and polished art. I talk of great original genius. Lady Di Beauclerc has made seven large drawings in soot-water for scenes of my *Mysterious Mother*. Oh! such drawings!" The drawings, which Walpole rated even higher than the *Decline and Fall*, were for his play, the plot of which is based on a double incest. Sixteen years before the play begins its chief character, the Countess of Narbonne, took the place of a girl she knew her son was about to seduce and now sixteen years later she fails to stop him from marrying their daughter.

5 Edward Gibbon (1737-1794), *The History of the Decline and Fall of the Roman Empire*, Vol. I. London, for W. Strahan and T. Cadell. a. May 1777, third edition, b. February 1776. FIRST EDITION.
(From the collection of George Edwards)

In the third edition of Vol. I, in response to suggestions from David Hume who liked Gibbon's history but not his book design, the notes were moved from the end of the volume to the bottom of the the page where cited and the number of the chapter was printed at the head of the margin; this arrangement was continued in Vols. II-VI. The third edition of Vol. I is the only part of the *Decline and Fall* that Gibbon revised after the publication of the first edition.

6 John Nichols (editor), *Gentleman's Magazine*. August 1776.
(From the Williams College Library)

The controversies over the *Decline and Fall* can be followed in the pages of the *Gentleman's Magazine*. From the first review, the magazine had little favorable to say: ". . . this too fashionable work . . . we cannot dismiss without expressing our surprise at the indiscriminate praise which has been lavished upon it by other reviewers." In August of 1788, a letter to the editor, signed "Eblanensis" challenged Gibbon to respond to letters, published six years earlier in the magazine in November 1782, defending the authenticity of the seventh verse the fifth chapter of the first epistle of St. John, signed "T" [Travis]. Richard Porson, a young classics scholar, came to Gibbon's defense with letters published in October and December 1788 and an additional five in 1789. (See ITEMS 38-44.)

7 Edward Gibbon (1737-1794), *A Vindication of Some Passages in the Decline and Fall of the Roman Empire*. London, for W. Strahan and T. Cadell, 1779. 8vo. FIRST EDITION.

CHAPTERS XV AND XVI, the last two chapters of Vol. I, gave a history of the rise and spread of Christianity that stirred up a storm of theological controversy in England. Gibbon stood above the fray: ". . . till Mr. Davis of Oxford presumed to attack not the faith, but the good faith of the historian. My *Vindication,* expressive less of anger than contempt. . . . " These two controversial chapters won the *Decline and Fall* a place on the *Index Librorum Prohibitorum,* the papal list of forbidden books. Thomas Bowdler, having completed a censored edition of Shakespeare suitable for family reading, proceeded to do the same for the *Decline and Fall;* Bowdler's edition (1826) among other omissions, leaves out chapters fifteen and sixteen altogether.

III • Gibbon's Biography

". . . I know that from my early youth I aspired to the character of an historian."
— Memoirs of My Life.

8 **Edward Gibbon (1737-1794), *An Essay on the Study of Literature.* Published originally in French (July 1761). London, for T. Becket and P. A. de Hondt, January 1764.**

The publisher arranged for this translation of Gibbon's first publication, *Essai sur l'étude de la littérature.* Gibbon was not pleased: ". . . the author (had his feelings been more exquisite) might have wept over the blunders and baldness of the English translation." Gibbon's compositions were in French until David Hume talked him out of it: "Why do you compose in French, and carry faggots into the wood, as Horace says with regard to Romans who wrote in Greek?" ". . . our solid and increasing establishments in America where we need less dread the inundation of Barbarians, promise a superior stability and duration to the English language." — from a letter addressed to Gibbon on October 24, 1767.

9 **Edward Gibbon (1737-1794), fragment of a draft in Gibbon's handwriting for *Memoirs of My Life*, circa 1790.**
(From the collection of George Edwards)

Gibbon's autobiography actually consisted of six drafts and miscellaneous notes and memoranda for an unfinished "memoirs of my life," which were edited into an "autobiography" and published in *Miscellaneous Works* by his friend and executor, Lord Sheffield. The text of this scrap was omitted from Lord Sheffield's first version of the *Memoirs* (1796) and is slightly different from the text that he included in his final version (1814), with the words in *italics* replaced by the words in [brackets].

". . . the Emperors of Germany and Kings of Spain have threatened the liberty of the old, and invaded the treasures of the new World.

14

The successors of Charles the fifth may disdain their *humble kins-men* [brethren] of England: but the *small volumes* [Romance] of Tom Jones, that exquisite picture of human *life* [manners], will survive the palace of the Escurial and the Imperial eagle of the house of Austria."

10 Henry Fielding (1707-1754), *The History of Tom Jones*. **London, for A. Millar, 1749. 6 vols. 12mo.** FIRST EDITION.

Gibbon enjoyed Fielding's novels. In addition to the mention in his autobiography of "the small volumes of Tom Jones, that exquisite picture of human life," he also refers to Fielding in footnote 13 of CHAP. XXXII of the *Decline and Fall*: "I am almost tempted to quote the romance of a great master, which may be considered as the history of human nature."

11 Lord Sheffield, editor, (1735-1821), *Miscellaneous Works of Edward Gibbon, Esq. with Memoirs of His Life and Writings, Composed by Himself: Illustrated from His Letters, with Occasional Notes and Narrative,* Vol. I. **London, for A. Strahan and T. Cadell, Jr., 1796.** FIRST EDITION.

"The engraving in the frontispiece is taken from the figure of Mr. Gibbon cut with scissors by Mrs. Brown. . . . The extraordinary talents of this lady have furnished as complete a likeness of Mr. Gibbon; as to person, face, and manner, as can be conceived." — Lord Sheffield, *Miscellaneous Works*.

". . . I drew my snuff box, rapped it, took snuff twice, and continued my discourse in my usual attitude of my body bent forwards, and my fore finger stretched out." — Gibbon in a letter to John Holroyd (later Lord Sheffield), May 1764.

12 James Boswell (1740-1795), *The Life of Samuel Johnson*. **London, H. Baldwin, 1791. 2 vols.** FIRST EDITION.

Boswell did not like Gibbon (or Adam Smith): "We talked of a work much in vogue at that time, written in a very mellifluous style, but which, under pretext of another subject, contained much artful infidelity. . . . I observed, that as he had changed several times — from the Church of England to the Church of Rome, — from the Church of Rome to infidelity, — I did not despair yet of seeing him a Methodist preacher. Johnson (laughing) 'It is said, that his range has been more extensive, and that he has once been Mahometan'...." — During a visit to Oxford, March 20, 1776.

13 Lord Byron (1788-1824), *Childe Harold's Pilgrimage*. London, for J. Murray, 1816. FIRST EDITION.

CANTO III.

"The other, deep and slow, exhausting thought,
And hiving wisdom with each studious year,
In meditation dwelt, with learning wrought,
And shaped his weapon with an edge severe,
Sapping a solemn creed with solemn sneer;
The lord of irony, —that master-spell,
Which stung his foes to wrath, which grew from fear,
And doom'd him to the zealot's ready Hell,
Which answers to all doubts so eloquently well."

IV · Gibbon's Library

"To a lover of books the shops and sales in London present irresistible temptations...." — Memoirs of My Life.

{Gibbon's library of six to seven thousand volumes was not as rich in early and rare editions as the Chapin's; actual editions owned by Gibbon are indicated in brackets; chapter and note (N.) references are to the *Decline and Fall*}

14 Gibbon's bookplates in a copy of a work on Roman taxation. Pieter Burmann (1668-1741), *Vectigalia populi Romani*. Leyden 1734. (From the collection of George Edwards)

The primitive looking label was the first mark of ownership added by Gibbon and the bookplate carrying the family arms (actually the family arms of an unrelated branch of the Gibbons of Kent) was used at a later date. After Gibbon's death in 1794, this book was bought with the greater part of his library, by William Beckford to give himself "something to read when I passed through Lausanne." (See also ITEM 37.)

"The mildness and precision of their [Trajan and the Antonines] laws ascertained the rule and measure of taxation, and protected the subject of every rank against arbitrary interpretations, antiquated claims, and the insolent vexation of the farmers of the revenue. (See Burman. de Vectigal.)" — CHAP. VI.N.III.

15 Homer (circa 850 BC?), Demetrius Chalcondyles, editor, (1423-1511), *Ποίησις ἅπασα.* Florence, Demetrius Damilas (printer) for Bernardo Nerli, 1488. 2 vols. {G's copy: 1525}

"Read and feel the xxiiid book of the Iliad, a living picture of manners, passions, and the whole form and spirit of the chariot race." — CHAP. XL.N.41. ". . . the Greek verses are harmonious, a dead language can seldom appear low or familiar; and at the distance of two thousand seven hundred years, we are amused with the primitive manners of antiquity." — CHAP. LV.N.68.

"The press of Aldus Manutius, a Roman, was established at Venice about the year 1494: he printed above sixty considerable works of Greek literature, almost all for the first time. . . . Yet his glory must not tempt us to forget, that the first Greek book, the Grammar of Constantine Lascaris, was printed at Milan in 1476; and that the Florence Homer of 1488 displays all the luxury of the typographical art." — CHAP. LXVI.N.116.

16 Herodotus (circa 484-430 BC), *Libri novem (Greek)*. Venice, Aldus Manutius, 1502. (Robert Hoe copy) {G's copy: 1763}

"There is not any writer who describes in so lively a manner as Herodotus, the true genius of Polytheism." — CHAP. II.N.3. "Procopius tells the story with the tone half skeptical, half superstitious, of Herodotus." — CHAP. XL.N.132. "Herodotus elegantly describes the strange effects of grief in another royal captive, Psammetichus of Egypt wept at the lesser, and was silent at the greatest of his calamities." — CHAP. XLI.N.31. "It will be a pleasure, not a task, to read Herodotus." — CHAP. XLII.N.I.

17 Aristotle (384-322 BC), *Opera (Greek)*. Venice, Aldus Manutius, 1495. 5 vols. (Robert Hoe copy) {G's copy: 1577}

"According to some, says Aristotle (as he is quoted by Julian) the form of absolute government . . . is contrary to nature. Both the

17

prince and the philosopher chuse, however, to involve this eternal truth in artful and laboured obscurity." — CHAP. XXII.N.70.

18 Cicero (106-43 BC), *De oratore*. Subiaco, Sweynheym & Pannartz, 1465. {G's copy: 1695}

"I read with application and pleasure *all* the Epistles, *all* the Orations. . . . Cicero in Latin and Xenophon in Greek are indeed the two ancients whom I would first propose to a liberal scholar, not only for the merit of their style and sentiments but for the admirable lessons which may be applied almost to every situation of public and private life." — *Memoirs of My Life.*

19 Suetonius (circa AD 69-122), *Vitæ Cæsarum*. Venice, N. Jenson, 1471. {G's copy: 1697}

"The former is confirmed by the diligent and accurate Suetonius, who mentions the punishment which Nero inflicted on the Christians. . . ." — CHAP. XVI.

"The Greek presses of Aldus and the Italians were confined to the classics of a better age." — CHAP. LXVIII.N.97. Until Greek type was available, a space was left in the printed text for a scribe to insert a Greek quotation. The Greek proverb, "Make haste slowly" [σπεῦδε βραδέως] inserted on this page of Jenson's Suetonius, along with the anchor and dolphin on the reverse of a *denarius* minted during the reign of the emperor Titus (AD 79-81) were the inspiration for Aldus's colophon. According to Suetonius, the two faults that Augustus condemned most strongly in a military commander were haste and recklessness, and he constantly quoted such Greek proverbs as "Make haste slowly," and "Better a safe commander than a bold one."

20 Tacitus (circa AD 56-120), *Germania*. Bologna, B. Azoguidus, 1472. {G's copy: 1627}

"Tacitus has employed a few lines, and Cluverius one hundred and twenty-four pages, on this obscure subject. The former discovers in Germany the gods of Greece and Rome. The latter is positive, that, under the emblems of the sun, the moon, and the fire, his pious ancestors worshipped the Trinity in unity." — CHAP. IX.N.62. "The revolution of ages may bring round the same calamities; but ages may revolve, without producing a Tacitus to describe them." — CHAP. XXXVI.N.IIO. "This deep disquisition fills only two pages; but they are the pages of Tacitus." — CHAP. XLIV.N.24.

21 Dionysius Cato? (William Caxton, translator), *Disticha de moribus ad filium*. Westminster, W. Caxton, after 23 December 1483. {G's copy: 1759}

Gibbon's copy was in Greek and Latin rather than in the English of Caxton's translation shown here. He also owned Joseph Scaliger's critique of this third or fourth century work. Joseph Justus Scaliger (1540-1609) was a French Huguenot whose classical scholarship was used by, and also amused Gibbon: "With respect to the time when these Roman games were celebrated, Scaliger, Salmasius, and Cuper, have given themselves a great deal of trouble to perplex a very clear subject." — CHAP. XII.N.99. "I leave Scaliger and Salmasius to quarrel about the origin of Cumæ, the oldest Greek colony in Italy, already vacant in Juvenal's time and now in ruins." — CHAP. XLIII.N.45.

22 Justinian (ad 482-565), *Institutiones*. Mainz, P. Schoeffer, 23 May 1476. {G's copy: 1753}

"The vain titles of the victories of Justinian are crumbled into dust: but the name of the legislator is inscribed on a fair and everlasting monument. Under his reign, and by his care, the civil jurisprudence was digested in the immortal works of the CODE, the PANDECTS, and the INSTITUTES: the public reason of the Romans has been silently or studiously transfused into the domestic institutions of Europe, and the laws of Justinian still command the respect or obedience of independent nations." — CHAP. XLIV.

23 Hernando Cortes (1485-1547), *La preclara narratione della Nuova Hispagna del mare oceano*. Venice, Bernardino de Viano de Lexona, 20 August 1524. {G's copy: 1778}

"Spain by a very singular fatality, was the Peru and Mexico of the old world. The discovery of the rich western continent by the Phoenicians, and the oppression of the simple natives, who were compelled to labour in their own mines for the benefit of strangers, form an exact type of the more recent history of Spanish America." — CHAP. VI.

24 Miguel de Cervantes (1547-1616), *Don Quixote*. Madrid, Iuan de la Cuesta, 1605, 1615. 2 vols. 1605, second edition; 1615, first edition. {G's copy: 1742}

"The Arabs traversed the province of La Mancha, which the pen of Cervantes has transformed into classic ground to the readers of every nation." — CHAP. LI.N.177.

25 William Shakespeare (1564-1616), *Mr. William Shakespeares Comedies, Histories, & Tragedies*. London, for W. Iaggard and E. Blount, 1623. FIRST FOLIO EDITION. {G's copy: 1765}

"Shakespeare had never read the poems of Gregory Nazianzen: he was ignorant of the Greek language; but his mother-tongue, the language of nature, is the same in Cappadocia and in Britain." — CHAP. XXVII.N.29. "If the reader will turn to the first scene of the first part of Henry the Fourth, he will see in the text of Shakespeare the natural feelings of enthusiasm; and in the notes of Dr. Johnson, the workings of a bigoted though vigorous mind, greedy of every pretence to hate and persecute those who dissent from his creed." — CHAP. LVIII.N.20.

26 [Blaise Pascal (1623-1662)], *Les provinciales*. Cologne, chez Pierre de la Vallée, 1657. FIRST EDITION. {G's copy: 1698}

"From the provincial letters of Pascal, which almost every year I have perused with new pleasure, I learned to manage the weapon of grave and temperate irony, even on subjects of Ecclesiastical solemnity." — *Memoirs of My Life*.

27 Isaac Newton (1642-1727), *Opticks*. London 1704. FIRST EDITION. {G's copy: 1704}

"The word ὃ (*which*) was altered to θεός (*God*) at Constantinople in the beginning of the sixth century . . . and this fraud, with that of the *three witnesses of St. John*, is detected by Sir Isaac Newton. I have weighed the arguments, and may yield to the authority of the first of philosophers, who was deeply skilled in critical and theological studies." — CHAP. XLVII.N.17. (See also ITEM 41.)

28 Pierre Bayle (1647-1706), *Dictionnaire historique et critique*. Amsterdam, P. Brunel, 1730. 4 vols. FOURTH EDITION. {G's copy: 1740}

"His critical Dictionary is a vast repository of facts and opinions; and he balances the *false* Religions in his skeptical scales till the opposite quantities (if I may use the language of Algebra) annihilate each other. 'I am most truly,' said Bayle, 'a protestant; for I protest indifferently against all Systems and all Sects.'" — *Memoirs of My Life.* "The sceptic of Rotterdam exhibits, according to his custom, a strange medley of loose knowledge, and lively wit." — CHAP. XXV.N.45.

29 [Abbé de la Bleterie (1696-1772)], *Vie de l'empereur Julien.* **Paris, chez Prault, 1735. 2 vols.** FIRST EDITION.
(From the collection of George Edwards) {G's copy: 1746}

"The *devout* Abbé de la Bleterie (Vie de Julien, p. 159.) is almost inclined to respect the *devout* protestations of a Pagan." — CHAP. XXII.N.12. "The chastity of Julian is confirmed by the impartial testimony of Ammianus and the partial silence of the Christians. Yet Julian ironically urges the reproach of the people of Antioch, that he *almost always* lay alone. This suspicious expression is explained by the Abbé de la Bleterie with candour and ingenuity." — CHAP. XXII.N.50.

30 [Samuel **Johnson** (1709-1784)], *A Dictionary of the English Language.* **London, W. Strahan, 1755. 2 vols.** FIRST EDITION. {G's copy: 1755}

"Dr. Johnson affirms, that *few* English words are of British extraction. Mr. Whitaker, who understands the British language, has discovered more than *three thousand.* . . . It is possible, indeed, that many of these words may have been imported from the Latin or Saxon into the native idiom of Britain." — CHAP. XXXVIII.N.144.

31 F.M.A. **Voltaire** (1694-1778), *Candide.* **[Geneva, Cramer] 1759.** FIRST EDITION. {G's copy: 1768}

Gibbon met Voltaire on his grand tour (1764) and later they were neighbors in Switzerland with Voltaire living at Ferney and Gibbon at Lausanne. Voltaire is mentioned about forty times in the footnotes of the *Decline and Fall*, e.g., "Voltaire, whose pictures are sometimes just, and always pleasing. . . ." "In his way, Voltaire was a bigot, an intolerant bigot. . . . " "Voltaire, as usual, prefers the Turks to the Christians. . . . "

32 [Benjamin Franklin (1706-1790)], *The Interest of Great Britain Considered.* London, for T. Becket, 1760. FIRST EDITION. {G's copy: 1760}

Franklin was passionate about science but otherwise he and Gibbon were alike in their distrust of fanaticism. In the winter of 1776, so the story goes, chance found them staying at the same inn in France. Franklin invited Gibbon to join him for dinner and an evening of conversation; Gibbon returned a note to the effect that although he respected Dr. Franklin's character, as a man and a philosopher, his principles would not allow him to sup with a revolutionary subject of his King. (In a letter to John Holroyd, dated June 16, 1777, after Gibbon had been in Paris for five weeks, he wrote that "I have dined *by accident* with Franklin. . . ." Apparently they did have dinner together after all.)

33 **William Blackstone (1723-1780), Commentaries on the Laws of England. Oxford, Clarendon Press, 1765-9. 4 vols.** FIRST EDITION. {G's copy: 1765-9}

"The Vinerian professorship [at Oxford] . . . has at least produced the excellent commentaries of Sir William Blackstone." — *Memoirs of My Life.* "In England, the oldest son alone inherits *all* the land, a law, says the orthodox judge Blackstone, unjust only in the opinion of younger brothers. It may be of some political use in sharpening their industry." — CHAP. XLIV.N.145.

34 [Samuel Johnson (1709-1784)], *Taxation No Tyranny.* London, for T. Cadell, 1775. {G's copy: 1775}

Both Johnson and Gibbons supported the British government against the American colonies:

"I took my seat at the beginning of the memorable contest between Great Britain and America; and supported with many a sincere and silent vote the rights, though not, perhaps, the interest of the mother country." — *Memoirs of My Life*, September 1774. "You have seen by the papers the unpleasant news from America . . . it was not an engagement, much less a defeat. The King's troops were ordered to destroy a magazine at Concord. They marched, did their business and returned, but they were frequently fired at from behind stone walls and from the windows in the Villages." — Gibbon in a letter to Edward Eliot, May 31, 1775, after the news of the battle of Lexington on April 19th had reached London on May 28th.

35 James Cook (1728-1779), *A Voyage to the Pacific Ocean in the Years 1776, 1777, 1778, 1779 and 1780.* London, H. Hughs, 1785. 3 vols. SEC-OND EDITION {G's copy: 1784}

"A second list . . . of modern English Books which ought to be in my library [to be reconstituted at Lausanne after his move there from London in September 1783] for myself and others; [Cadell] will get them in *sheets* which will diminish the carriage and enable me to bind them uniformly. . . . You hesitated if I am not mistaken about Coxe [*Travels into Poland, Russia, Sweden and Denmark*] and Cooke's Voyages; the former as a subscriber I have paid for already; and shall be disappointed if I do not find them both in the boxes, the omission of the latter would be the most serious as I understand that the price at first high is considerably enhanced." — Gibbon in a letter to Peter Elmsley, a bookseller in London, September 26, 1784.

36 [Thomas Jefferson (1743-1826)], *Notes on the State of Virginia.* [Paris] 1782. FIRST EDITION {G's copy: 1787}

Jefferson published his "Notes on Virginia" just as the "War" was ending.

"Peace will be proclaimed tomorrow; odd! As War was never de-clared. The buyers of stock seem as indifferent as yourself about the definitive Treaty." — Gibbon in a letter to Lord Sheffield, September 9, 1783 (Preliminaries of peace had been signed in January but the treaty that concluded the war with America, France and Spain was not signed until September 2, 1783.)

37 [William Beckford (1760-1844)], *An Arabian Tale translated by S. Henley.* London, for J. Johnson, 1786.

William Beckford, a wealthy English dilettante, purchased Gibbon's library at Lausanne. Although Beckford wanted to have Gibbon's books, he apparently did not think much of the *Decline and Fall.* (See Beckford's note under Biographical Quotations circa 1790.) In 1787 Beckford published *Vathek,* an imaginary tale, in French. This English translation by Dr. Samuel Henley had, con-trary to Beckford's wish, been published first, anonymously, in 1786.

V · Gibbon's Scholarship

".. . some angry letters from Mr. Travis . . . made me personally responsible for condemning with the best critics the spurious text of the three heavenly witnesses." — Memoirs of My Life.

The spurious text of the three heavenly witnesses . . .

38 Edward Gibbon (1737-1794), *The History of the Decline and Fall of the Roman Empire*, Vol. III. London, for W. Strahan and T. Cadell, March 1781. FIRST EDITION.

> "The memorable text which asserts the unity of the THREE who bear witness in heaven is condemned by the universal silence of the orthodox fathers, ancient versions, and authentic manuscripts. . . . After the invention of printing, the editors of the Greek Testament yielded to their own prejudices, or those of the times;[119] and the pious fraud, which was embraced with equal zeal at Rome and Geneva, has been infinitely multiplied in every country and every language of modern Europe."

> [119] "The three witnesses have been established by the prudence of Erasmus; the honest bigotry of the Complutensian editors; the typographical fraud, or error, of Robert Stephens in the placing a chotchet; and the deliberate falsehood, or strange misapprehension of Theodore Beza." — CHAP. XXXVII.

The universal silence of authentic manuscripts . . .

39 Desiderius Erasmus, editor and translator, (1467-1536), *Novvm instrumentum omne* (New Testament in Greek and Latin). Basle, J. Froben, 1516. 2 vols. FIRST EDITION.

In 1516 Erasmus and his printer, Johann Froben, published the New Testament in Greek for the first time, using the cursive Greek fonts of Aldus Manutius and the Latin translation of Erasmus. In the first epistle of St. John, the fifth chapter, the seventh verse, Erasmus left out a text that had been used to support the doctrine of the unity of the Trinity because, as he explained in the accompanying volume of notes, this phrase was not present in any of the Greek manuscripts that he had examined. The Latin Vulgate Bible reads:

Quoniam tres sunt qui testimonium dant *in caelo:*
Pater: Verbum: & Spiritus sanctus: & hi tres unum sunt.
Et tres sunt qui testimonium dant in terra:
Spiritus: & aqua: & sanguis:
& hi tres unum sunt.

[For there are three that bear record *in heaven,*
the Father, the Word, and the Holy Ghost: & these three are
one.
And there are three that bear record in earth,
the Spirit, and the water, and the blood:
and these three are one.]

Leaving out the words in italics above, the "spurious text,"
Erasmus's version in both Greek and Latin reads:

[For there are three that bear record,
the spirit, and the water, and the blood:
and these three are one.]

The prudence of Erasmus . . .

40 Hagia Petra Monastery, *Codex Theodori* (New Testament in Greek on vellum). Mount Athos 1295.

After the publication of his second edition in 1519, Erasmus was attacked by Stunica (Diego de Zuñiga), one of the editors of the Complutensian Polyglot Bible, which had been printed (1514-1517) in Spain but not yet released for circulation. In response to his criticism, Erasmus explained that if he had found the controversial text in at least one of the manuscripts he had examined, he would have included it. One manuscript with the text was discovered at Oxford and this was communicated to Erasmus. Erasmus *prudently* made a tactical retreat by putting the disputed text in his third edition of February 1522. The Oxford manuscript has since been dated to about 1520 while earlier manuscripts, like this one from Mount Athos of 1295, all have the shorter text:

ὅτι τρεῖς εἰσιν οἱ μαρτυροῦντες,
τὸ πνεῦμα, καὶ τὸ ὕδωρ, καὶ τὸ αἷμα,
καὶ οἱ τρεῖς εἰς τὸ ἕν εἰσιν.

[For there are three that bear record,
the spirit, and the water, and the blood:
and these three are one.]

The honest bigotry of the Complutensian editors . . .

41 Francisco Jiménez de Cisneros, Cardinal Ximenes, patron, (1436-
1517); Diego Lopez de Zuñiga et al., editors; Arnaldo Guillen de
Broca, printer; *The Complutensian Polyglot Bible*. Alcalá de
Henares, printed 1514-1517, published 1522. 6 vols. FIRST EDITION.

The Complutensian Polyglot finally appeared in circulation in 1522
with a version of the three witnesses side by side in Greek and
Latin. The text printed as the Greek version of 1 JOHN v.7 had been
translated from the Latin Vulgate without a word of explanation.
Gibbon forgave this lack of candor as "the honest bigotry of the
Complutensian editors" for they *believed* that their Latin text was
infallible. The editors did deviate slightly from the Latin Vulgate,
which created the opportunity to bring in the authority of St.
Thomas, he of little Greek, as a witness for the doctrine of the
Trinity. As Newton [one of Gibbon's "best critics"] pointed out,
they cleverly used the marginal note on their change to the *Latin*
version to give authority to their newly minted *Greek*.

*The typographical fraud, or error, of Robert Stephens in the placing a
crotchet . . .*

42 Robert Estienne, editor and printer, (1503-1559), Τῆς Καινῆς
Διαθήκης ἅπαντα (New Testament in Greek). Paris 1550.

Robert Estienne (Stephens) used the Greek fonts of Claude
Garamond to produce his folio New Testament of 1550. Notations
in the margins refer to variant readings that appear in the
Complutensian Bible (α) and in fifteen Greek manuscripts. The
text itself is based on Erasmus's fourth edition of 1527, for which
Erasmus had a copy of the Complutensian as one of the texts to use
in revising his third edition. At 1 JOHN v.7, Estienne marked `*in
heaven*` to indicate that these words were not in the seven manu-
scripts noted in the inner margin:

ὅτι τρεῖς εἰσιν οἱ μαρτυροῦντες ʿἐν τῷ οὐρανῷ,ʾ
ὁ πατήρ, ὁ λόγος, καὶ τὸ ἅγιον πνεῦμα· καὶ οὗτοι οἱ
τρεῖς ἕν εἰσι.
καὶ τρεῖς εἰσιν οἱ μαρτυροῦντες ἐν τῇ γῇ,
τὸ πνεῦμα, καὶ τὸ ὕδωρ, καὶ τὸ αἷμα·
καὶ οἱ τρεῖς εἰς τὸ ἕν εἰσι.

[For there are three that bear record ʿ*in heaven*,ʾ
the Father, the Word, and the Holy Ghost: and these three are one.
And there are three that bear record in earth,
the Spirit, and the water, and the blood:
and these three are one.]

The "crotchet" [ʾ] should have been placed twenty-two words later after *earth*ʾ in order to include all of the words that are absent from the manuscripts. Estienne's "typographical fraud, or error," may have been a prudent way of avoiding a charge of heresy, in the years after the death of François I in 1547, when France became considerably less tolerant. In any event in the next year, 1551, Estienne moved from Paris to Geneva to become the printer for John Calvin.

The deliberate falsehood, or strange misapprehension, of Theodore Beza …

43 Theodore Beza, editor and translator, (1519-1605), *The New Testament in English*. Dortrecht, I. Canin, 1603.

In 1548 Theodore Beza, a French theologian, married his mistress and joined the church of Calvin at Geneva. Beza published a number of editions of the New Testament, which were used by the translators for the King James Version of the Bible. Beza's printed text was based on Estienne's of 1550 and his "falsehood, or strange misapprehension," was to misrepresent the manuscript basis for interpolations such as the Three Heavenly Witnesses. What Beza suggested was that since Estienne had found 1 JOHN v.7 defective in the seven manuscripts listed in the margin of item 42, he must have found the text complete in the other eight. In fact, the seven manuscripts cited as lacking the Heavenly Witnesses were the only ones containing the canonical epistles, leaving only the Complutensian as an authority.

After the invention of printing . . . the pious fraud . . . has been infinitely
multiplied in every country and every language of modern Europe.

44 Translators for King James, committee, (1604-1611), *The Holy Bible.* London, R. Barker, 1611. FIRST EDITION.

In the King James Version (KJV) following Beza, the parentheses, placed around the questionable passage by Tyndale and Coverdale, were dropped and the Three Witnesses were given a headline at the upper right. The KJV reads:

7 For there are three that beare record in heaven,
  the Father, the Word, and the holy Ghost: and these three are one.
8 And there are three that beare witnesse in earth,
  the Spirit, and the Water, and the Blood,
  and these three agree in one.

It was the history and the scholarship of this corruption of Scripture that Gibbon summarized in a footnote of the third volume of the *Decline and Fall* published in 1781. Richard Porson replied to Gibbon's critics, in *Gentleman's Magazine,* during 1788-89. In 1881, after another one hundred years of controversy, the Three Heavenly Witnesses were banished to the footnotes of the Greek New Testament.

VI • Gibbon's Roman Portraits

"My English text is chaste, and all licentious passages are left in the obscurity of a learned language." — Memoirs of My Life.

45 **Augustus** (EMPEROR 27 BC—AD 14). *Denarius.*

"A cool head, an unfeeling heart and a cowardly disposition, prompted him, at the age of nineteen, to assume the mask of hypocrisy, which he never afterwards laid aside. His virtues, and even his vices, were artificial; and according to the various dictates of his interest, he was at first the enemy, at last the father, of the Roman world." — *Decline and Fall,* CHAP. III. "His will was the law of mankind, but, in the declaration of his laws, he borrowed the voice of the senate and people. . . . In his dress, his domestics, his titles, . . . Augustus maintained the character of a private Roman; his most artful flatterers respected the secret of his absolute and perpetual monarchy." — *Decline and Fall*, CHAP. XLIX.

46 Nerva (EMPEROR AD 96-98). *Denarius.*

"Nerva had scarcely accepted the purple from the assassins of Domitian, before he discovered that his feeble age was unable to stem the torrent of public disorders, which had multiplied under the long tyranny of his predecessor. His mild disposition was respected by the good; but the degenerate Romans required a more vigorous character. . . . Though he had several relations, he fixed his choice on a stranger. He adopted Trajan, then about forty years of age, and who commanded a powerful army in the Lower Germany; and immediately, by a decree of the senate, declared him his colleague and successor in the empire." — *Decline and Fall*, CHAP. III.

47 Trajan (EMPEROR AD 98-117). *Denarius.*

"It is sincerely to be lamented, that whilst we are fatigued with the disgustful relation of Nero's crimes and follies, we are reduced to collect the actions of Trajan from the glimmerings of an abridgement, or the doubtful light of a panegyric. There remains, however, one panegyric far removed beyond the suspicion of flattery. Above fifty years after the death of Trajan, the senate, in pouring out the customary acclamations of the accession of a new emperor, wished that he might surpass the felicity of Augustus, and the virtue of Trajan." — *Decline and Fall*, CHAP. III.

48 Hadrian (EMPEROR AD 117-138). *Denarius.*

"Under [Hadrian's] reign, the empire flourished in peace and prosperity. He encouraged the arts, reformed the laws, asserted military discipline, and visited all his provinces in person. His vast and active genius was equally suited to the most enlarged views, and the minute details of civil policy. But the ruling passions of his soul were curiosity and vanity. As they prevailed, . . . Hadrian was, by turns, an excellent prince, a ridiculous sophist, and a jealous tyrant. The general tenor of his conduct deserved praise for its equity and moderation. Yet in the first days of his reign, he put to death four consular senators, his personal enemies, and men who had been judged worthy of empire; and the tediousness of a painful illness rendered him, at last, peevish and cruel." — *Decline and Fall*, CHAP. III.

49 **Antoninus Pius** (EMPEROR AD 138-161). *Denarius.*

"Antoninus diffused order and tranquility over the greatest part of the earth. His reign is marked by the rare advantage of furnishing very few materials for history; which is, indeed, little more than the register of the crimes, follies, and misfortunes of mankind. In private life, he was an amiable, as well as a good man. The native simplicity of his virtue was a stranger to vanity or affectation. He enjoyed, with moderation, the conveniencies of his fortune, and the innocent pleasures of society; and the benevolence of his soul displayed itself in a cheerful serenity of temper." — *Decline and Fall,* CHAP. III.

50 **Marcus Aurelius** (EMPEROR AD 161-180). *Denarius.*

"The mildness of Marcus, which the rigid discipline of the Stoics was unable to eradicate, formed, at the same time, the most amiable, and the only defective, part of his character. His excellent understanding was often deceived by the unsuspecting goodness of his heart. . . . His excessive indulgence to his brother, his wife, and his son, exceeded the bounds of private virtue, and became a public injury. . . . Faustina, the daughter of Pius and the wife of Marcus, has been as much celebrated for her gallantries as for her beauty. The grave simplicity of the philosopher was ill-calculated to engage her wonton levity, or to fix that unbounded passion for variety, which often discovered personal merit in the meanest of mankind." — *Decline and Fall,* CHAP. IV.

51 **Septimus Severus** (EMPEROR AD 193-211). *Denarius.* [also **Julius Cæsar** (100-44 BC)].

"The uncommon abilities and fortune of Severus have induced an elegant historian to compare him with the first and greatest of the Cæsars. The parallel is, at least, imperfect. Where shall we find, in the character of Severus, the commanding superiority of soul, the generous clemency, and the various genius, which could reconcile and unite the love of pleasure, the thirst of knowledge, and the fire of ambition?" — *Decline and Fall,* CHAP. V.

"Though it is not, most assuredly, the intention of Lucan, to exalt the character of Cæsar, yet the idea he gives of that hero, in the tenth book of the Pharsalia, where he describes him, at the same time, making love to Cleopatra, sustaining a siege against the power of Egypt, and conversing with the sages of the country, is, in reality, the noblest panegyric." — *Decline and Fall,* CHAP. V.N.41.

"The contemporaries of Severus, in the enjoyment of the peace and glory of his reign, forgave the cruelties by which it had been introduced. Posterity, who experienced the fatal effects of his maxims and example, justly considered him as the principal author of the decline of the Roman empire." — *Decline and Fall,* CHAP. V.

52 Gordian II (CO-EMPEROR, 36 days, AD 238). *Denarius.*

"His manners were less pure, but his character was equally amiable with that of his father. Twenty-two acknowledged concubines, and a library of sixty-two thousand volumes, attested the variety of his inclinations; and from the productions which he left behind him, it appears that the former as well as the latter were designed for use rather than for ostentation." — *Decline and Fall,* CHAP. VII. "By each of his concubines, the younger Gordian left three or four children. His literary productions, though less numerous, were by no means contemptible." — *Decline and Fall,* CHAP. VII.N.19.

53 Aurelian (EMPEROR AD 270-275). *Antoninianus.* [also Zenobia, (QUEEN OF PALMYRA 267-272)].

"The reign of Aurelian lasted only four years and about nine months; but every instant of that short period was filled by some memorable achievement. He put an end to the Gothic war, chastised the Germans who invaded Italy, recovered Gaul, Spain, and Britain out of the hands of Tetricus, and destroyed the proud monarchy which Zenobia had erected in the East, on the ruins of the afflicted empire. . . ."

"Zenobia is perhaps the only female, whose superior genius broke through the servile indolence imposed on her sex by the climate and manners of Asia. She claimed her descent from the Macedonian kings of Egypt, equaled in beauty her ancestor Cleopatra, and far surpassed that princess in chastity and valour. Zenobia was esteemed the most lovely as well as the most heroic of her sex. She was of a dark complexion (for in speaking of a lady, these trifles become important). . . . She was not ignorant of the Latin tongue, but possessed in equal perfection the Greek, the Syriac, and the Egyptian languages." — *Decline and Fall,* CHAP. XI.

54 Diocletian (EMPEROR AD 285-305). *Argenteus.*

"The valour of Diocletian was never found inadequate to his duty or to the occasion; but he appears not to have possessed the daring and generous spirit of a hero, who courts danger and fame, disdains artifice, and boldly challenges the allegiance of his equals. His abilities were useful rather than splendid; a vigorous mind, improved by the experience and study of mankind . . . and above all, the great art of submitting his own passions, as well as those of others, to the interest of his ambition. . . . Like Augustus, Diocletian may be considered as a founder of a new empire. Like the adopted son of Cæsar, he was distinguished as a statesman rather than as a warrior; nor did either of those princes employ force, whenever their purpose could be effected by policy." — *Decline and Fall*, CHAP. XIII.

55 Julian (EMPEROR AD 361-363). *Reduced siliqua.*

"The generality of princes, if they were stripped of their purple, and cast naked into the world, would immediately sink to the lowest rank of society, without a hope of emerging from their obscurity. But the personal merit of Julian was, in some measure, independent of his fortune. . . . His genius was less powerful and sublime than that of Cæsar; nor did he possess the consummate prudence of Augustus. The virtues of Trajan appear more consistent. Yet Julian sustained adversity with firmness, and prosperity with moderation. . . . Even faction, and religious faction, was constrained to confess, with a sigh, that the apostate Julian was a lover of his country, and that he deserved the empire of the world." — *Decline and Fall*, CHAP. XXII.

APPENDICES

On Reading Gibbon's *Decline and Fall*

THE BEST EDITION for reading Gibbon's *Decline and Fall* is: David Womersley (editor), *Edward Gibbon: The History of the Decline and Fall of the Roman Empire.* In three volumes. London: Allen Lane, The Penguin Press, 1994.

The Penguin Press edition is available in paperback (Penguin Classics, about $20 per volume from Amazon.com) and has excellent indices.

The current Modern Library edition in three volumes is based on the Heritage Press edition, which has a reader-friendly format but does not include all of Gibbon's notes; for example, footnotes 23-26 in CHAPTER XL on the youthful career of Justinian's Empress Theodora are omitted: "The satirical historian [Procopius] has not blushed[23] to describe the naked scenes which Theodora was not ashamed to exhibit in the theater.[24] After exhausting the arts of sensual pleasure,[25] she most ungratefully murmured against the parsimony of Nature;[26] but her murmurs, her pleasures, and her arts must be veiled in the obscurity of a learned language."

On the other hand, in the Folio Society edition, Felipe Fernández-Armesto has translated the learned Greek and Latin of these footnotes into plain English.

Chronology

1737	8 May (27 April old style), birth of Edward Gibbon.
1746	December, death of his mother.
1752	April, enters Magdalen College, Oxford.
1753	Converted to Roman Catholicism; sent to Lausanne.
1754	Returns to Protestantism.
1755	Father remarries.
1757	Meets and falls in love with Suzanne Curchod.
1758	5 May, returns to England.
	24 August, breaks engagement to Suzanne Curchod.
1760-62	Active duty in Hampshire militia.
1761	Publishes *Essai sur l'étude de la littérature.*
1763-65	Grand tour of Paris, Lausanne, and Italy; August 1763, meets John Baker Holroyd, later Lord Sheffield; 15 October 1764, supposed date of Gibbon's epiphany on the Capitoline Hill.
1767	Begins and then abandons a history of Swiss liberty.
1770	Publishes *Critical Observations on the Sixth Book of the Aeneid;* 12 November, his father dies.
1773	February, starts writing *Decline and Fall.*
1774	Elected Member of Parliament for Liskeard.
1776	17 February, publishes Volume I of *Decline and Fall.*
	3 June, second edition of 1500 copies, 750 sold in three days.
	4 June, begins to write the first chapter of Volume II. American Declaration of Independence; Gibbon supports Lord North.
	16 October, an anonymous pamphlet published attacking Vol. I.
	31 October, Dr. Watson's "Apology for Christianity" against the *Decline and Fall,* published.
1777	May-October, visits Paris.
1778	Gibbon votes with Fox in Parliament; France allied with America.
	Henry Edwards Davis attacks Gibbon's honesty and reliability.
1779	Publishes his *Vindication;* appointed to Board of Trade.
1780	Loses parliamentary seat for Liskeard.
1781	Elected Member of Parliament for Lymington. Publishes Volumes II and III of the *Decline and Fall.*
1782	North government falls; Board of Trade abolished.
	Letters signed 'T' [Travis] in *Gentleman's Magazine* attack Gibbon for condemning the "three heavenly witnesses."
1783	Writes Volume IV of *Decline and Fall;* moves to Lausanne to share a house with Georges Deyverdun.

1787	In England to supervise publication of final volumes of *Decline and Fall* (Volume VI finished in Switzerland on 27 June 1787.)
1788	8 May, dinner in London to celebrate publication of *Decline and Fall*, Volumes IV-VI, on Gibbon's fifty-first birthday.
	30 July arrives in Lausanne; begins autobiography.
	August, letter signed 'Eblanensis' in *Gentleman's Magazine* challenges Gibbon to reply to Travis's letters of 1782.
	October, Richard Porson comes to Gibbon's defense with a devastating reply to Travis in a series of letters published by *Gentleman's Magazine*.
1789	Deyverdun dies; Gibbon stays on in Lausanne.
1793	June, in England following the death of Lady Sheffield.
1794	16 January, Gibbon dies in London.
1796	Lord Sheffield publishes his version of Gibbon's autobiography. Lord Sheffield sells Gibbon's books to William Beckford for £950.

Biographical Quotations: Lytton Strachey

"Happiness is the word that immediately rises to the mind at the thought of Edward Gibbon: and happiness is its widest connotation — including good fortune as well as enjoyment. Good fortune, indeed, followed him from the cradle to the grave in the most tactful way possible; occasionally it appeared to fail him; but its absence always turned out to be a blessing in disguise. Out of a family of seven he alone had the luck to survive — but only with difficulty; and the maladies of his childhood opened his mind to the pleasures of study and literature. His mother died; but her place was taken by a devoted aunt, whose care brought him through the dangerous years of adolescence to a vigorous manhood. His misadventures at Oxford saved him from becoming a don. His exile to Lausanne, by giving him a command of the French language, initiated him into European culture, and at the same time enabled him to lay the foundations of his scholarship. His father married again; but his stepmother remained childless and became one of his dearest friends. He fell in love; the match was forbidden; and he escaped the dubious joys of domestic life with the future Madame Necker. While he was allowed to travel on the Continent, it seemed doubtful for some time whether his father would have the resources or the generosity to send him over the Alps into Italy. His fate hung in the balance; but at last his father produced the necessary five hundred pounds and, in the autumn of 1764, Rome saw her historian. His father died at exactly the right moment, and left him exactly the right amount of money.

"At the age of thirty-three Gibbon found himself his own master, with a fortune just sufficient to support him as an English gentleman of leisure and fashion. For ten years he lived in London, a member of Parliament, a placeman, and a diner-out, and during those ten years he produced the first three volumes of his History. After that he lost his place, failed to obtain another, and, finding his income unequal to his expenses, returned to Lausanne, where he took up his residence in the house of a friend, overlooking the Lake of Geneva. It was the final step in his career, and no less fortunate than all the others. In Lausanne he was rich once more, he was famous, he enjoyed a delightful combination of retirement and society. Before another ten years were out he had completed his History; and in ease, dignity, and absolute satisfaction his work in this world was accomplished." — Lytton Strachey, *Portraits in Miniature* (1931).

Biographical Quotations: On Himself

"He is described, by Petrarch and Boccacce, as a man of diminutive stature, though truly great in discernment, sure of learning and genius; of a piercing discernment though of a slow and painful elocution. For many ages (as they affirm) Greece had not produced his equal in the knowledge of history, grammar, and philosophy; and his merit was celebrated in the attestations of the princes and doctors of Constantinople." — Probably a slight sketch of himself in the portrait of the early Renaissance scholar Barlaam [AD 1339]. *Decline and Fall*, CHAPTER LXVI, 1788.

"To the University of Oxford I acknowledge no obligation; and she will as willingly renounce me for a son, as I am willing to disclaim her for a mother. I spent fourteen months (1752-53) at Magdalen College (it is vulgarly pronounced Maudlin); they proved the fourteen months the most idle and unprofitable of my whole life." — *Memoirs of My Life.*

". . . on my return to England, I soon discovered that my father would not hear of this strange alliance, and that without his consent I was myself destitute . . . I sighed as a lover, I obeyed as a son. . . ." — *Memoirs of My Life* on breaking his engagement to Suzanne Curchod, the future Mme. Necker and mother of Mme. de Staël (circa 1758).

"It has always been my practice to cast a long paragraph in a single mould, to try it by my ear, to deposit it in my memory, but to suspend action of the pen till I had given the last polish to my work." — *Memoirs of My Life.*

". . . I have described the triumph of barbarism and religion; and I can only résumé, in a few words, their real or imaginary connection with the ruin of ancient Rome." — *Decline and Fall*, CHAP. LXXI.

"It was among the ruins of the Capitol, that I first conceived the idea of a work which has amused and exercised near twenty years of my life, and which, however inadequate to my own wishes, I finally deliver to the curiosity and candour of the public." — last lines of the *Decline and Fall*, June 27, 1787, *Decline and Fall*, CHAP. LXXI.

"I consider Mr. Porson's answer to Archdeacon Travis as the most acute and accurate piece of criticism which has appeared since the days of Bentley . . . I am satisfied with his honourable testimony to my attention, diligence, and accuracy — those humble virtues which Religious zeal has most audaciously denied. The sweetness of his praise is tempered by a reasonable mixture of acid." — *Memoirs of My Life* on Richard Porson's reply to Travis in *Gentleman's Magazine,* October 1788 — August 1789.

"I will that my funeral be regulated with the strictest simplicity; and that if I should die abroad, my remains, instead of being transported to England, be decently interred at the place of my decease — Shall I be accused of vanity if I add that a monument is superfluous?" — *Will of Edward Gibbon,* made in 1788.

". . . concerning the future fate of my library . . . besides the pecuniary advantage of my poor heirs, I consider a public sale as the most laudable method of disposing of it. From such sales my books were chiefly collected, and when I can no longer use them they will be again culled by various buyers according to their wants and means. . . ."- Gibbon in a letter to Lord Sheffield, May 1792.

"When I contemplate the common lot of mortality, I must acknowledge that I have drawn a high prize in the lottery of life." — *Memoirs of My Life.*

Biographical Quotations: 18th Century

"Whether I consider the dignity of your style, the depth of your matter, or the extensiveness of your learning, I must regard the work as equally the object of esteem, and I own that, if I had not previously had the happiness of your personal acquaintance, such a performance from an Englishman in our age would have given me some surprise." — David Hume in a letter to Gibbon, March 18, 1776.

"Si vous avez moins de précision que cet historien [Tacitus], en revanche vous avez cent fois plus d'idées, et de variétiés dans les idées. On voit qu'il a été le modèle et peut-être la source de votre ouvrage, mais c'est une source qui s'est grossie de tous les torrents de pensées qui ont coulé dans tous siècles . . . Les seuls philosophes lisent Tacite, vous serez lu de tout le monde." [If you have less precision than Tacitus, you have one-hundred times more ideas, and more variety in your ideas. He seems to have been the model and perhaps the source of your work, but a source enlarged by a torrent of thoughts from every century . . . Only philosophers read Tacitus; you will be read by everyone.] — Mme. Necker, *née* Suzanne Curchod, September 1776.

"King George in a fright Lest Gibbon should write
The story of Britain's disgrace,
Thought no way so sure
His pen to secure
As to give the historian a place." — attributed to Charles James Fox

"Another damned thick, square book! Always scribble, scribble, scribble! Eh! Mr. Gibbon?" — Duke of Gloucester, brother of King George III, on being presented with Volume II, circa March 1781.

"Je vous rend grâce d'avoir rempli un intervalle immense dans l'histoire et d'avoir jeté sur le chaos ce pont qui joint le monde ancien au monde moderne." [I thank you for having filled an immense gap in history and for having thrown across chaos this bridge that links the ancient and modern worlds.] — Mme. Necker *née* Suzanne Curchod, April 21, 1781.

"The time is not far distant, Mr. Gibbon, when your almost ludicrous self-complacency, your numerous, and sometimes apparently willful mistakes, your frequent distortion of historical Truth to provoke a gibe, or excite a sneer at everything most sacred and venerable, your ignorance of the oriental languages, your limited and far from acutely critical knowledge of the Latin and the Greek, and in the midst of all the prurient and obscene gossip of your notes — your affected moral purity perking up every now and then from the corrupt mass like artificial roses shaken off in the dark by some Prostitute on a heap of manure, your heartless skepticism, your unclassical fondness for meretricious ornament, your tumid diction, your monotonous jingle of periods, will be still more exposed and scouted than they have been. Once fairly kicked off from your lofty, bedizened stilts, you will be reduced to your just level and true standard." — William Beckford, 1759-1844, note in his copy of the *Decline and Fall,* circa 1790s.

"A less pardonable fault is that rage for indecency which pervades the whole work, but especially the last volumes.. . . " — Richard Porson in the preface to his *Letters to Mr. Travis,* 1790.

"Began Gibbon last evening. I find he requires as much study and attention as Horace; so I shall not rank the reading of him among amusements. Skated an hour; fell twenty times, and find the advantage of a hard head." — Aaron Burr, "Plan of a Journal" in a letter to his daughter Theodosia, December 16, 1793.

"Gibbon's style is detestable; but it is not the worst thing about him." — Samuel Taylor Coleridge, *Table Talk,* August 15, 1833.

"It is this *indirectness* of observation, then, which forms the soul of the style of Gibbon, of which the apparently pompous phraseology is the body. Another peculiarity, somewhat akin to this, has less reason to recommend it, . . . I mean the coupling in one sentence matters that have but a very shadow of connexion. For instance — 'The Life of Julian, by the Abbé de la Bleterie, first introduced me to the man and to the times, *and* I should be glad to recover my first essay on the truth of the miracle which stopped the building of the temple at Jerusalem.' This laughable Gibbonism is still a great favourite with the *stellæ minores* of our literature." — Edgar Allan Poe, *American Museum,* February 1839.

"It is melancholy to say it, but the chief, perhaps the only, English writer who has any claim to be considered an ecclesiastical historian, is the unbeliever Gibbon." — Cardinal Newman, *Essay on the Development of Christian Doctrine,* 1845.

"Gibbon still represents the most important work ever to be written on Roman history, offering a fine résumé and telling characterizations." — Theodor Mommsen, circa 1885.

". . . Gibbon's is the worst English that was ever written by an educated Englishman." — John Ruskin in a reply to a survey about Sir John Lubbock's selection of the 'best hundred books' for the working men wishing to educate themselves, 1886.

"Someone had told me that my father had read Gibbon with delight; that he knew whole pages of it by heart, and that it had greatly affected his style of speech and writing. So without more ado I set upon the eight volumes of Dean Milman's edition of Gibbon's *Decline and Fall of the Roman Empire.* . . . All through the long glistening middle hours of the Indian day, from when we quitted stables till the evening shadows proclaimed the hour of Polo, I devoured Gibbon . . . I scribbled all my opinions on the margins of the pages, and very soon found myself a vehement partisan of the author against the disparagements of his pompous-pious editor. I was not even estranged by his naughty footnotes." — Winston Churchill, *My Early Life,* circa 1896.

"... we must consider Gibbon's zealous distrust of zeal as an essential and most suggestive characteristic of the *Decline and Fall*." — J.B. Bury, introduction to his edition of the *Decline and Fall*, 1896.

"Adams never tired of quoting the supreme phrase of his idol Gibbon, before the Gothic cathedrals: 'I darted a contemptuous look on the stately monuments of superstition.' Even in the footnotes of his history, Gibbon never inserted a bit of humor more human than this, and one would have paid largely for a photograph of the fat little historian, on the background of Notre Dame of Amiens, trying to persuade his readers — perhaps himself — that he was darting a contemptuous look on the stately monument, for which he felt in fact the respect which every man of his vast study and active mind always feel before objects worthy of it." — Henry Adams, *The Education of Henry Adams*, 1905.

Biographical Quotations: 20th Century

"As a master of historical technique, Gibbon is without equal ... Accurate in every statement of his work, there has lived no individual writer responsible for a greater volume of inferential falsehood than he.... Of all histories, that of Constantinople is least capable of biographical treatment. Following his method there might be compiled with equal regard for fact and disdain of truth, a chronicle of the American continent from the sexual shortcomings of transatlantic presidents, fortified by an implicit belief in the veracity of the Hearst press." — Robert Bryan, *The Byzantine Achievement*, 1929.

"Happiness is the word that immediately rises to the mind at the thought of Edward Gibbon.... His father died at exactly the right moment, and left him exactly the right amount of money." — Lytton Strachey, *Portraits in Miniature*, 1931.

"'Yet, upon the whole, the *History of the Decline and Fall* seems to have struck root, both at home and abroad, and may, perhaps, a hundred years hence still continue to be abused.' So Gibbon wrote in the calm confidence of immortality; and let us confirm him in his own opinion of his book by showing, in the first place, that it has one quality of permanence—that it still excites abuse." — Virginia Woolf, *The Historian and "The Gibbon,"* 1937.

". . . his eventual choice of language was dramatically justified when an odd volume of the *Decline and Fall* — finding its way into a tract in the heart of North America — fell into the hands of a certain young backwoodsman [Abraham Lincoln], unversed in any tongue but his native English, who was eagerly educating himself with aid of the few books that he had managed to acquire." — Arnold J. Toynbee, *A Study of History, Vol.V: Edward Gibbon's Choice of Linguistic Vehicle*, 1939.

"Thus his *Decline and Fall* is both a complex and vivid picture of the Middle Ages from a certain point of view and a unique self-portrait of the eighteenth-century mind." — Arnaldo Momigliano, *Gibbon's Contribution to Historical Method*, 1954.

"What Gibbon learned from Tacitus, then, was a kind of discriminating disenchantment . . . It was this temper that Gibbon glimpsed in Tacitus when he singled him out as perhaps the only ancient who could truly be called a philosophical historian." — Peter Gay, *Style in History*, 1974.

"The author of the fifteenth and sixteenth chapters of the *Decline and Fall of the Roman Empire* could be expected to have a natural affinity for an emperor who tried to undo the work of Constantine. Gibbon's extensive treatment of Julian spans chapters 19, 22, 23, and most of 24 of the *Decline and Fall*, and its amplitude emphasizes the significance he attached to a ruler whose uncontested reign lasted but a year and a half. Gibbon's portrait of Julian . . . is admiring though critical at times." — G.W. Bowersock, *Gibbon and Julian*, 1976.

"Nowadays, historians' arguments must still stride forward or totter backward on their footnotes. But the lead of official prose has replaced the gold of Gibbon's classic oratory."—Anthony Grafton, *The Footnote: A Curious History*, 1997.

What book—except the Bible—has been most important to you? "Read Edward Gibbon's 'Decline and Fall of the Roman Empire' during Navy flight training. It contains themes and lessons that we must draw upon in conducting modern politics and statecraft."— Senator John McCain, quoted in *The Wall Street Journal*, January 3, 2000.

The Bogus Trinity at Trinity[*]

A Footnote On a Gloss

IN THE THIRD VOLUME of *The History of the Decline and Fall of the Roman Empire*, Edward Gibbon used a footnote[1] to summarize the history of a spurious text in the New Testament known as "the three heavenly witnesses." The text of the first letter of John, Chapter V, verse 7 (JOHN v. 7) was important to the Christian church because it was a biblical text that could be cited in defense of the doctrine of the Trinity. By the time Gibbon was writing, this text had been sanctified by the King James Authorized Version of the Bible. His footnote rekindled the controversy over the *Decline and Fall*, which had arisen five years earlier when the first volume was published in 1776, concerning its history of Christianity. In particular Gibbon was attacked by Archdeacon Travis in series of letters published in the *Gentleman's Magazine*. A young classical scholar named Richard Porson rose to Gibbon's defense:

> It is scarcely necessary to tell the reader, that in the years 1516 and 1519 Erasmus published his first and second editions of the Greek Testament, both [of] which omitted the three heavenly witnesses. That having promised Lee to insert them in his text, if they were found in a single Greek manuscript he was soon informed of the existence of such a manuscript in England, and consequently inserted 1 JOHN v. 7 in his third edition, 1522. That this manuscript after a profound sleep of two centuries, has at last been found in the library of Trinity College, Dublin. That the Complutensian edition, which was not published till 1522, though it professes to be printed in 1514, has the seventh and eighth verses patched up from the modern Latin manuscripts and the final clause of the eighth verse, which is omitted in its proper place, transferred to the end of the seventh.[2]

*Reprinted from *The Grolier Club Iter Hibernicum*, New York 1998.

1. Chapter XXXVII, footnote 120 [119]; ed. David Womersley, London, Allen Lane: The Penguin Press, 1994, II, p. 443: "The three witnesses have been established in our Greek Testaments by the prudence of Erasmus; the honest bigotry of the Complutensian editors.. . . "
2. Richard Porson, *Letters to Mr. Archdeacon Travis, in answer to his Defence of the Three Heavenly Witnesses, 1 John V. 7*. London 1790, pp. i-ii.

THE BOGUS TRINITY AT TRINITY: *A Famous Manuscript Fraud in the Trinity College Library. The spurious text of 1 John v. 7 appears in the last five lines of folio 439 recto* (TCD MS 30) *italicized in* [ ] *below.*

ὅτι τρεῖς εἰσιν οἱ μαρτυ-
ροῦντες, [*ἐν τῷ οὐρανῷ, πατὴρ, λόγος, καὶ πνεῦμα ἅγιον,
καὶ οὗτοι οἱ τρεῖς ἕν εἰσι. καὶ τρεῖς εἰσιν οἱ μαρτυροῦντες ἐν τῇ γῇ,*] πνεῦμα, ὕδωρ, καὶ αἷμα. εἰ τὴν
μαρτυρίαν τῶν ἀνθρώπων λαμβάνομεν, ἡ μαρτυρία τοῦ

The background of this controversy was as follows. From Gutenberg onwards, the Bible printed in Latin had contained the following text at 1 JOHN v. 7 —brackets, italics, and translation added:

Quoniam tres sunt qui testimonium dant [*in caelo: pater: verbum: et spiritus sanctus:*
et hi tres unum sunt. Et tres sunt qui testimonium dant in terra:]
spiritus: aqua:
et sanguis{: et hi tres unum sunt}.

(For there are three that bear witness [*in heaven, the Father, the Word, and the Holy Ghost:*
and these three are one. And there are three that bear witness in earth,]
the spirit, the water,
and the blood{: and these three are one}.)

When Erasmus was preparing his Latin translation of the New Testament with the original Greek in a parallel column to provide support, he was unable to find any Greek manuscript that included the text in italics. Therefore he left this passage out of his edition (Basle, Froben, February 1516) and explained in an appendix why he had done so.[3] Edward Lee, a sycophant of Henry VIII and later Archbishop of York, disparaged Erasmus for this omission. In March 1519, Froben printed a second, revised edition of Erasmus' New Testament in Greek & Latin—still without the disputed text of 1 JOHN v. 7. This was the edition used by Martin Luther for his German translation and by William Tyndale for his English one. Lee attacked Erasmus again, this time in print, as did Stunica, a principal editor of the Complutensian Polyglot Bible.[4] Earlier, from 1514 to 1517, the Complutensian had been printed at Alcalá in Spain (the ancient Roman city of Complutum) at the initiative and expense of Francisco Jiménez de Cisneros, Cardinal Ximenes, but had not yet been released for publication.

Erasmus answered Lee that he had consulted more than seven Greek manuscripts, and found it wanting in them all; and that if he could have found it in any one manuscript, he would have followed that in favor of the Latin.[5]

3. D. Erasmus, *Annotationes in Novum Testamentum*, Basle, Froben, February 1516, p. 618.
4. Edward Lee, *Annotationes in annotationes Novi Testamenti Desiderii Erasmi*, Paris 1520; Stunica (Diego Lopez de Zuamenti *Annotationes contra Erasmum Roterodamum in defensionem tralationis Novi Testamenti*, Alcalá 1520.
5. D. Erasmus, *Responsio ad annotationes Eduardi Lei*, Antwerp 1520: ". . . tantum illud dicam, mihi diversis temporibus plura fuisse Exemplaria quam septem [i.e., Greek], nec in ullo horum repertum, quod in nostris [i.e., Latin] legitur. Quod si mihi contigisset unum Exemplar, in quo fuisset quod nos legimus, nimirum illinc adjecissem quod in cæteris

During the year 1520, Erasmus was notified that such a manuscript had been found at Oxford. Erasmus, who never saw the Oxford manuscript, smelled something fishy and suspected that it was a contemporary one corrected by the Latin. Nonetheless, by that time he was under pressure to prove himself an orthodox Christian as compared with the heretic Luther. Erasmus prudently made a tactical retreat by putting the disputed text in his third edition of February 1522.[6] Around 1700 when Sir Isaac Newton studied this "corruption of scripture," he concluded that a trick had been played on Erasmus, especially since the manuscript could no longer be found in England.[7] Later in the eighteenth century the Oxford manuscript was discovered in the library of Trinity College, Dublin, where it was subsequently much visited. In his defense of Gibbon, Porson had concluded that the Oxford/Dublin manuscript was probably written about the year 1520 and placed at Oxford to deceive Erasmus. By 1881, after another hundred years of controversy, biblical scholars had become convinced that Erasmus, Newton, Gibbon, and Porson were right and that the manuscript

---

aberat. Id quia non contigit, quod solum licuit feci, indicavi quid in Græcis codicibus minus esset." (In Erasmus's *Opera Omnia*, Lugduni Batavorum 1703-1706, volume IX, p. 275.) Note that Porson took poetic license in telling the story, which has become a legend, that Erasmus had "promised Lee to insert [the three heavenly witnesses] in his text, if they were found in a single Greek manuscript" and had kept his promise when one was produced. In fact, what Erasmus gave, in his reply to Lee, was not a promise but an account of what he had done in preparing his first and second editions.

6. D. Erasmus, *Annotationes in Novum Testamentum*, third edition, Basle, Froben, February 1522, p. 770: "Ex hoc igitur codice Britannico reposuimus, quod in nostris dicebatur deesse; ne cui sit ansa calumniandi. Tametsi suspicor codicem illum ad nostros esse correctum." [Now that this Codex Britannicus has been called to my attention, to avoid their slanders, I will include it in mine. Nevertheless I suspect this codex to have been corrected to the Latin version.] H.J. de Jonge, a recent editor of Erasmus' collected works, suggests that this annotation does not necessarily mean that Erasmus suspected that the Codex Britannicus had been written especially to induce him to insert the disputed text; de Jonge would rather that this annotation implies that Erasmus suspected only that it was a manuscript of recent origin which had been made to conform to the Latin Vulgate. (H.J. de Jonge, "Erasmus and the Comma Johanneum," *Ephermerides Theologicae Lovanienses 56* (1980), pp. 381-389.) Under either interpretation, Erasmus suspected that the Codex Britannicus (Minuscule 61) was not a legitimate witness for the text of the New Testament. Although unconvinced of its merit, Erasmus was under tremendous pressure to eliminate any suspicion of unorthodoxy; given the need to protect his good name from calumnies, this "made to order" manuscript was successfully used to force him to insert the three witnesses in his third edition.

7. Sir Isaac Newton, *An Historical Account of Two Notable Corruptions of Scripture, Exactly reprinted from Bishop Horsley's Edition of Sir Isaac Newton's Works, vol. V. 1785;* (first published incompletely at London in 1754) London 1830, pp. 42-43: ". . . since he was only told of such a manuscript, in the time of the controversy between him and Lee, and never saw it himself, I cannot forbear to suspect, that it was nothing but a trick put upon him. . . ."

was a sixteenth century forgery.[8] No earlier Greek manuscript with this text has ever been found; and the three heavenly witnesses have been banished from the Greek New Testament and its translations. The earliest citation of the three witnesses is a Latin treatise from the third century.[9] It was probably written as a marginal gloss on a Latin Bible from whence it crept into the text.

THE COMPLUTENSIAN POLYGLOT finally appeared in circulation in 1522. In the New Testament volume a modified version of the disputed text had been printed in Greek and Latin, with a note, which appeals to St. Thomas Aquinas for the authority of the modified text. The Complutensian was a landmark of scholarship and printing—six stately folio volumes finely printed in the original biblical languages of Hebrew, Aramaic, and Greek, with accompanying translations, dictionaries, grammars, and Latin versions arranged for comparison. *It was also a splendid fraud!*

Firstly, since a manuscript did not exist to provide the basis for the text printed as the Greek version of 1 JOHN v. 7, it must have been translated into Greek from the Latin version; but unlike the editions of Erasmus there was not a word of explanation. Gibbon forgave this lack of candor as "the honest bigotry of the Complutensian editors." They *believed* that their Latin text was infallible.

Secondly, in the preface to the Complutensian, the editors stated that Pope Leo X had lent Cardinal Ximenes some manuscripts from the Vatican Library; and that breathings and accents had been deliberately omitted for the Greek type face used to print the New Testament on the model of old manuscripts and monuments at Rome. This suggested that the manuscripts used for the Greek text, and as a model for the type font, might also be ancient. Indeed they succeeded in fooling Robert Proctor, the authority on early printing of Greek.[10] However, the handsome

---

8. B.F. Westcott and F.J.A. Hort, *The New Testament in the Original Greek: Appendix*, Cambridge and London 1881, p. 106: "The evidence as enlarged by Mill and Wetstein was rigorously examined by Porson *(Letters to Travis)* in 1790."

9. Augustinus Merck S.J., *Novum Testamentum: Græce et Latine*, tenth edition, Rome 1984: Earliest witness for the Clementine Vulgate text of John v. —*Liber de Rebaptismate*, circa AD 250.

10. Kennerly M. Woody, "A Note on the Greek Fonts of the Complutensian Polyglot," *Papers of the Bibliographical Society of America*, LXV (1971), pp. 143-149: ". . . the 'manuscript origin' of the Complutensian Greek font belongs to a well-populated world of historical myth."

Complutensian type was more likely modeled on Nicolas Jenson's Greek font, cut at Venice in the 1470s, than on an early manuscript.[11] Moreover, the manuscripts used for the Greek New Testament were not particularly old or distinguished[12] — apparently the editors were engaged in puffing in their preface.

Finally, because much was at stake, the editors dared to deviate from the printed version of the Latin Vulgate Bible, by leaving out the second {: et hi tres unum sunt}. This change created the opportunity to bring in the authority of St. Thomas, he of little Greek, as a witness for the doctrine of the Trinity. As Newton pointed out, they cleverly used the marginal note on their change to the *Latin* version to give authority to their newly minted *Greek*.[13] This change was not adopted by the Vatican in later editions of the Vulgate. Was it a remarkable coincidence that the publication of the Complutensian was delayed until after Erasmus had inserted the Trinitarian verse into his third edition?

D URING OUR VISIT to Dublin the present writer could not resist looking up this bit of *Gibboniana* in the Trinity College Library. After a brief search in assorted catalogues, the manuscripts librarian identified the manuscript in question and made a date for a viewing the next morning. The return visit had to be brief because the Grolier itinerary did not allow a lot of time for research. In the event it was well worth the detour of twenty minutes. In *Minuscule 61* (TCD MS 30), as the manuscript is known,[14] the paper leaf containing the forged text is discolored from use, at the hands of learned clergymen, and has been varnished for preservation so that it now stands out from all the rest of the octavo codex, which is a complete copy of the New Testament in Greek.

How did this fraudulent manuscript find its way from Oxford to Trinity College, Dublin? Some research on our return to New York re-

11. Victor Scholderer, *Greek Printing Types, 1465-1927,* London 1927, pp. 9-10: ". . . there can be little doubt that its designer had Jenson's Greek and kindred fonts in mind as well."

12. T.H. Darlowe & H.F. Moule, *Historical Catalogue of the Printed Editions of Holy Scripture,* London 1903. Ancient Greek No. 1517: "The text of the N.T. was based on comparatively late MSS. None of Ximenes' MSS now preserved at Madrid contains the Greek Testament. Neither of the two Greek MSS mentioned as having been borrowed from the Vatican contains any part of the N.T." "There is no evidence that Codex Vaticanus, or any other MS of high antiquity or first-rate importance was used."

13. Sir Isaac Newton, *An Historical Account of Two Notable Corruptions of Scripture . . .* , pp. 45-47: "I startle at the marginal note in this place in the cardinal's edition . . . ."

14. Constantin von Tischendorf and Casper René Gregory, *Novum Testamentum Græce: Prolegomena,* Leipzig 1890, minuscule No. 61, pp. 478-479: "Vidi 25 Maii 1883."

vealed that it was first noticed in 1520 by a Franciscan monk at Oxford who probably copied the codex himself and forged 1 John v. 7 in Greek as a word for word translation from a Latin manuscript.[15] It ended up in the library of James Ussher, Archbishop of Armagh, who had a reputation ('learned to a miracle') for encyclopedic erudition in the field of theological controversies, for which he built a collection of rare books and manuscripts.

One of his many publications, a chronology of the Old Testament, fixed the date of the creation of the world at 4004 BC, a date which is perhaps now discredited. He visited England frequently, where he met Thomas Bodley and William Camden and pursued his book collecting; he lived there in exile following the great rebellion of 1641 in Ireland. The manuscript in question was collated by Archbishop Ussher for the production (1652-1657) of Walton's Polyglot Bible[16] in which he was mentioned as one of the consulting editors. After Ussher's death in 1656 his daughter offered his library for sale; the sale was preempted by Cromwell for purchase by the state; and eventually, in 1661, the library of around 10,000 volumes was deposited at Trinity College, Dublin as the gift of Charles II. Thus a bogus Trinity became part of the library of Trinity College.[17]

George Edwards

15. J. Rendel Harris, *The Origin of the Leicester Codex of the NT,* London 1887, pp. 40-56: ". . . we have the good fortune to know the names probably of nearly every person through whose hands the MS has passed."
16. Orlando T. Dobbin, *The Codex Montfortianus,* London 1854, p. 20: "[Archbishop Ussher's] collation was in all likelihood completed in 1653, before the first volume of the Polyglot appeared."
17. *Dictionary of National Biography; Encyclopædia Britannica,* Eleventh Edition; *Treasures of the Mind,* Catalogue of a Trinity College Dublin Quatercentenary Exhibition, London 1992, "James Ussher."